Grade 1 Level 1 Early elemer

MW01000707

Improve your sight-reading!

Paul Harris

For online audio of all the pieces scan the QR code
or go to fabermusic.com/content/audio

FABER *ff* MUSIC

Practice chart

	Comments (from you, your teacher or parent)	Done!
Stage 1		
Stage 2		
Stage 3		
Stage 4		
Stage 5		
Stage 6		
Stage 7		
Stage 8		
Stage 9		

Teacher's name _____

Telephone _____

Many thanks to Jean Cockburn, Claire Dunham, Graeme Humphrey
and Diana Jackson for their invaluable help, and particular
thanks to Lesley Rutherford whose editorial skills and perpetual
encouragement went far beyond the call of duty.

© 2008 by Faber Music Ltd.
This edition first published in 2018 by Faber Music Ltd.
Bloomsbury House, 74–77 Great Russell Street, London WC1B 3DA
Music setting by Graham Pike
Cover and page design by Susan Clarke
Cover illustration by Drew Hillier
Printed in England by Caligraving Ltd
All rights reserved

ISBN10: 0-571-53301-9 (US edition 0-571-53311-6)
EAN13: 978-0-571-53301-5 (US edition 978-0-571-53311-4)

To buy Faber Music publications or to find out about the full range of titles available
please contact your local music retailer or Faber Music sales enquiries:
Faber Music Ltd, Burnt Mill, Elizabeth Way, Harlow CM20 2HX
Tel: +44 (0) 1279 82 89 82 Fax: +44 (0) 1279 82 89 83
sales@fabermusic.com   fabermusic.com

Introduction

Being a good sight-reader is so important and it needn't be difficult! If you work through this book carefully – always making sure that you really understand each exercise before you play it you'll never have problems learning new pieces or doing well at sight-reading in exams!

Using the workbook

1 Rhythmic exercises

Make sure you have grasped these fully before you go on to the melodic exercises: it is vital that you really know how the rhythms work. There are a number of ways to do the exercises, several of which are outlined in Stage 1. Try them all out. Can you think of more ways to do them?

2 Melodic exercises

These exercises use just the notes and rhythms for the Stage, and also give some help with fingering. If you want to sight-read fluently and accurately, get into the simple habit of working through each exercise in the following ways before you begin to play it:

- Make sure you understand the rhythm and counting. Clap the exercise through.
- Look at the shape of the tune, particularly the highest and lowest notes. Which finger do you need to start on to be able to play it? The exercises have this fingering added to get you started.
- Try to hear the piece through in your head. Always play the first note to help.

3 Prepared pieces

Work your way through the questions first, as these will help you to think about or 'prepare' the piece. Don't begin playing until you are pretty sure you know exactly how the piece goes.

4 Going solo!

It is now up to you to discover the clues in this series of practice pieces. Give yourself about a minute and do your best to understand the piece before you play. Check the rhythms and hand position, and try to hear the piece in your head. Always remember to feel the pulse and to keep going steadily once you've begun.

The **online audio** is for you to listen to *after* you have performed any sight-reading piece. Use it to check whether you have understood the rhythm and overall feel and style of the piece correctly.

Good luck and happy sight-reading!

Terminology:
Bar = measure

Stage 1

Rhythmic exercises

Always vary the way you do the rhythmic exercises. Here are a few ideas:
• Tap the pulse with your right foot (sometimes use your left foot!) and clap the rhythm.
• Tap the pulse with one hand and the rhythm with the other (swap hands!).
• Tap the pulse with your foot and play the rhythm on a note (either hand).
• Tap the pulse with your foot and make up a tune to fit the rhythm.
Before you begin each exercise count two bars in; the first out loud and the second silently.

4   Now write your own exercise and then clap it.

Melodic exercises

Before playing this first melodic exercise, write down the rhythm on the line underneath. The first bar is done for you. Then clap it.

Prepared pieces

1 How many beats are there in each bar? What will you count?

2 What is the key? Play the scale (or microscale*).

3 Look for the highest and lowest notes and check your fingering.

4 Can you spot any repeated patterns – rhythmic or melodic?

5 How will you put character into this piece?

6 Try to hear the music (melody and rhythm) in your head before you begin.

March

1 How will you count this piece?

2 Tap the rhythm then hear the rhythm silently in your head.

3 What is the key? Play the scale (or microscale).

4 Can you spot any repeated patterns – rhythmic or melodic?

5 How will you put character into this piece?

6 Try to hear the music in your head.

Gently

* See page 40 for details.

Going solo!

Don't forget to prepare each piece carefully before you play it.

Stage 2

Small leaps

Rhythmic exercises

Don't forget to count two bars in!

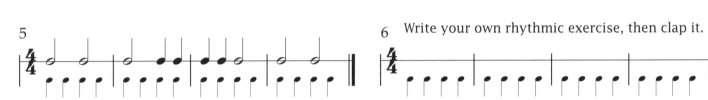

6 Write your own rhythmic exercise, then clap it.

Melodic exercises

Prepared pieces

> **1** How many beats is each 𝅗𝅥 worth?
>
> **2** What will you count? Tap the rhythm of the piece. Now hear the rhythm in your head.
>
> **3** What is the key? Play the scale (or microscale).
>
> **4** Can you spot any repeated patterns – rhythmic or melodic?
>
> **5** How will you put character into this piece?
>
> **6** Try to hear the music in your head before you begin.

Skipping

> **1** What will you count? Tap the rhythm of the piece. Now hear the rhythm in your head.
>
> **2** Say the letter names of each note. Play the scale (or microscale).
>
> **3** Look for the highest and lowest notes and check your fingering.
>
> **4** Can you spot any repeated patterns – rhythmic or melodic?
>
> **5** How will you put character into this piece?
>
> **6** Try to hear the music in your head before you begin.

Calmly

Going solo!

Stage 3

$\frac{3}{4}$ 𝅗𝅥.

G major

Rhythmic exercises

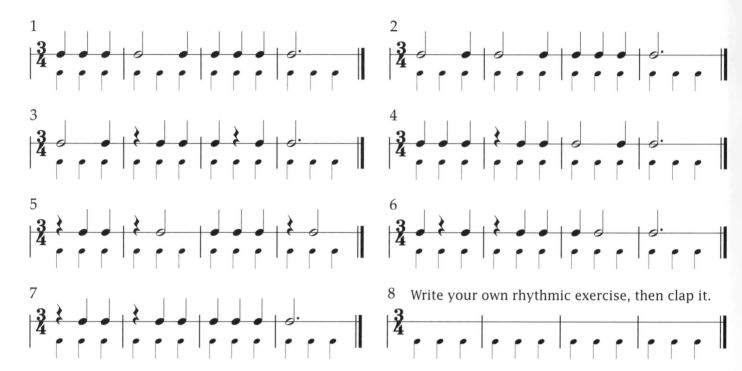

1

2

3

4

5

6

7

8 Write your own rhythmic exercise, then clap it.

Melodic exercises

1

2

3

Prepared pieces

1 What is the key of this piece? Play the scale (or microscale).

2 What will you count? Tap the rhythm of the piece. Now hear the rhythm in your head.

3 Look for the highest and lowest notes and check your fingering.

4 Can you spot any repeated patterns – rhythmic or melodic?

5 How will you put character into this piece?

6 Try to hear the music in your head before you begin.

Waltz-time

1 What will you count? Tap the rhythm of the piece. Now hear the rhythm in your head.

2 What is the key? Play the scale (or microscale).

3 How many F sharps are there?

4 What does *mf* (*mezzo forte*) mean?

5 How will you put character into this piece?

6 Try to hear the music in your head before you begin.

Allegro

Going solo!

Don't forget to prepare each piece carefully before you play it.

Stage 4

Rhythmic exercises

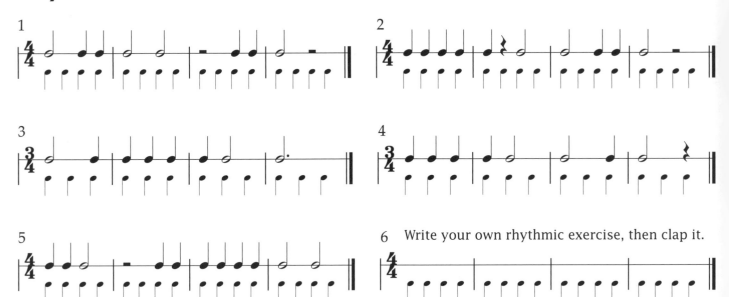

1

2

3

4

5

6   Write your own rhythmic exercise, then clap it.

Melodic exercises

When using both hands, you need to position them correctly
before you begin.

1

2

3

Prepared pieces

> **1** What is the key of this piece? Play the scale (or microscale) in both hands.
>
> **2** Say the names of all the notes. Where is the biggest leap?
>
> **3** What will you count? Tap the rhythm of the piece. Now hear the rhythm in your head.
>
> **4** Look for the highest and lowest notes and check your fingering.
>
> **5** How will you put character into this piece?
>
> **6** Try to hear the music in your head before you begin.

> **1** What is the key of this piece? Play the scale (or microscale) in both hands.
>
> **2** How many intervals of a third can you spot?
>
> **3** What will you count? Tap the rhythm of the piece. Now hear the rhythm in your head.
>
> **4** Compare the rhythm of bar 1 to the rhythm of bar 2.
>
> **5** How will you put character into this piece?
>
> **6** Try to hear the music in your head before you begin.

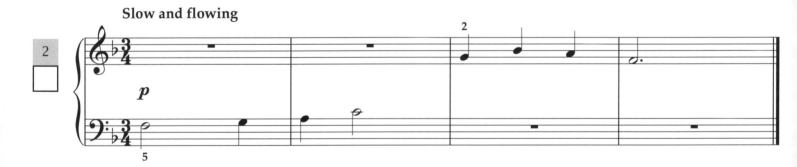

Going solo!

Stage 5

Rhythmic exercises

8   Write your own rhythmic exercise, then clap it.

Melodic exercises

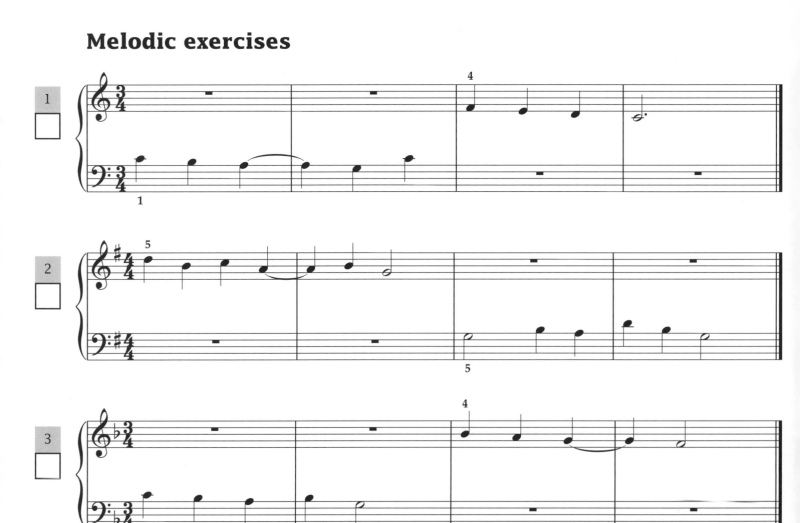

Prepared pieces

1 What is the key of this piece? Play the scale (or microscale) in both hands.

2 What is a tie? Can you find any here?

3 What will you count? Tap the rhythm of the piece. Now hear the rhythm in your head.

4 Can you spot any repeated patterns – rhythmic or melodic?

5 How will you put character into this music?

6 Try to hear the music in your head before you begin.

1 What is the key of this piece? Play the scale (or microscale) in both hands.

2 Look for the highest and lowest notes and check your fingering.

3 What will you count? Tap the rhythm of the piece. Now hear the rhythm in your head.

4 What particular pattern do you see in bars 1 and 2?

5 How will you put character into this piece?

6 Try to hear the music in your head before you begin.

Going solo!

Stage 6

2/4 and ♪♪
A minor
Phrasing

Rhythmic exercises

Melodic exercises

As you get to the end of a phrase make sure that you are
looking ahead to see what comes next – notes and rhythm.

Prepared pieces

1 What is the key of this piece? Play the scale (or microscale) in both hands.

2 What will you count? Tap the rhythm, then hear the rhythm in your head.

3 What is the opening interval? What is the connection with the final bar?

4 Can you spot any repeated patterns – rhythmic or melodic?

5 How will you put character into this piece?

6 Try to hear the music in your head before you begin.

1 What will you count? Tap the rhythm of the piece. Now hear the rhythm in your head.

2 What is the key? Play the scale (or microscale) in both hands.

3 How is it like a conversation?

4 Why are the dynamic levels important?

5 How will you put character into this piece?

6 Try to hear the music in your head before you begin.

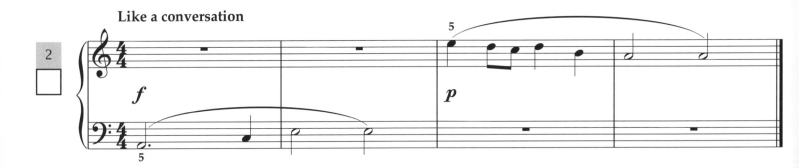

Going solo!

Stage 7

Rhythmic exercises

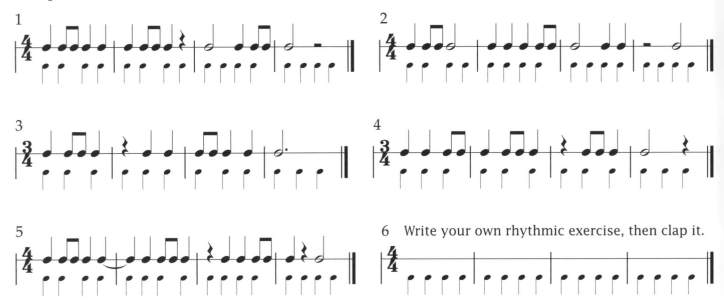

6   Write your own rhythmic exercise, then clap it.

Melodic exercises

You'll find lots of markings on the music now. Staccatos and accents, and in the Prepared pieces and Going solo sections, dynamic markings too. Do your best to bring these to life!

Prepared pieces

1 What is the key of this piece? Play the scale (or microscale) in both hands.

2 What will you count? Tap the rhythm, then hear the rhythm in your head.

3 Can you spot any repeated patterns – rhythmic or melodic?

4 How will you play the accented notes ♩ and the staccato notes ♩ ?

5 How will you use the dynamics to put character into this piece?

6 Try to hear the music in your head before you begin.

1 What is the key of this piece? Play the scale (or microscale) in both hands.

2 What will you count? Tap the rhythm, then hear the rhythm in your head.

3 Can you spot any repeated patterns – rhythmic or melodic?

4 Look at the first two bars for a few moments. Now play them from memory.

5 How will you put character into this piece?

6 Try to hear the music in your head before you begin.

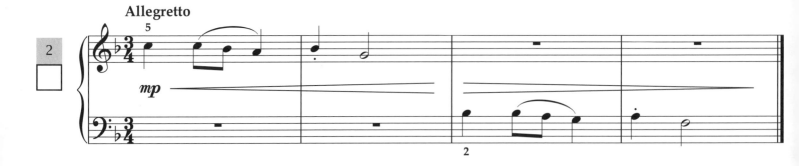

Going solo!

Don't forget to prepare each piece carefully before you play it.

Stage 8

D minor

Rhythmic exercises

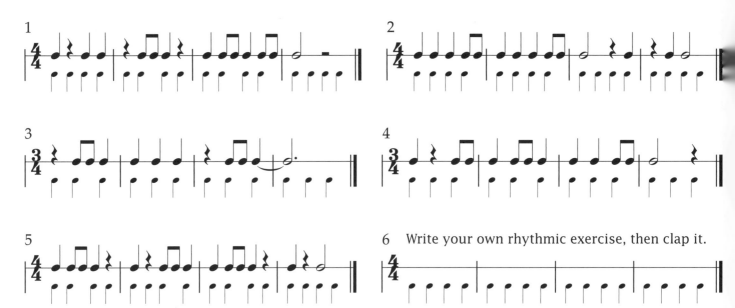

6 Write your own rhythmic exercise, then clap it.

Melodic exercises

Prepared pieces

1 What is the key of this piece? Play the scale (or microscale).

2 What will you count? Tap the rhythm, then hear the rhythm in your head.

3 Can you spot any repeated patterns – rhythmic or melodic?

4 Which finger will you use for the first note in each phrase?

5 How will you put character into this piece?

6 Try to hear the music in your head before you begin.

1 What is the key of this piece? Play the scale (or microscale).

2 What will you count? Tap the rhythm, then hear the rhythm in your head.

3 Can you spot any repeated patterns – rhythmic or melodic?

4 What are the clues to the character of this piece?

5 Look at the first bar for a few moments and then play it accurately from memory.

6 Try to hear the music in your head before you begin.

Going solo!

Stage 9

Rhythmic exercises

Melodic exercises

Make up your own tempo marking for each of the next nine pieces.
For example, Cheerfully, Sadly, Gracefully or Grumpily! Play it through
first, thinking about the character. Then decide on its marking.

Prepared pieces

1 What is the key of this piece? Play the scale (or microscale) in both hands.

2 What will you count? Tap the rhythm, then hear the rhythm in your head.

3 Can you spot any repeated patterns – rhythmic or melodic?

4 What do you notice about the dynamic shape?

5 How will you put character into this piece?

6 Try to hear the music in your head before you begin.

1 What is the key of this piece? Play the scale (or microscale) in both hands.

2 What will you count? Tap the rhythm, then hear the rhythm in your head.

3 Can you spot any repeated patterns – rhythmic or melodic?

4 Think carefully about the fingering in bars 6 and 7.

5 What speed will you play it? What will the character be?

6 Try to hear the music in your head before you begin.

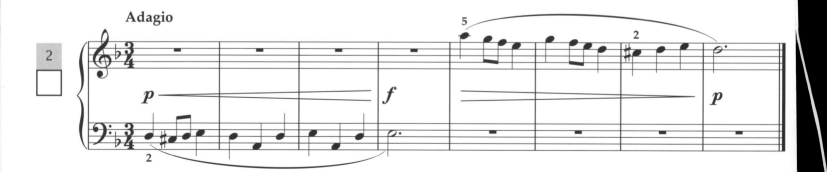

Going solo!

The golden rules

A sight-reading checklist

Before you begin to play a piece at sight, always consider the following:

1 Look at the time signature and decide how you will count the piece.

2 Look at the key signature and find the notes which need raising or lowering.

3 Notice patterns – especially those based on scales and arpeggios.

4 Check the fingering and hand position for each hand.

5 Notice any markings that will help you convey the character.

6 Count at least two bars in.

When performing a sight-reading piece

1 Keep feeling the pulse.

2 Keep going at a steady tempo.

3 Ignore mistakes.

4 Look ahead – at least to the next note.

5 Keep your hands in position on the keyboard.

6 Play musically, always trying to convey the character of the music.

Look at each piece for about 30 seconds and try to feel that you are understanding what you see (just like reading these words).

Don't begin until you think you are going to play the piece accurately.

Microscales

If you don't know the whole scale, just the first five notes or even just
the first three notes will do! Both patterns will give a good feel of the key.

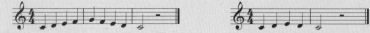